Animals
Sharks

by Nick Rebman

FOCUS READERS

www.focusreaders.com

Focus Readers is distributed by North Star Editions:
sales@northstareditions.com | 888-417-0195

Produced for Focus Readers by Red Line Editorial.

Photographs ©: wildestanimal/Shutterstock Images, cover, 1; weera bunnak/Shutterstock Images, 4; Ramon Carretero/Shutterstock Images, 7, 16 (top right); Derek Heasley/Shutterstock Images, 9, 16 (top left); frantisekhojdysz/Shutterstock Images, 11; VisionDive/Shutterstock Images, 13; Martin Prochazkacz/Shutterstock Images, 15, 16 (bottom right); Jag_cz/Shutterstock Images, 16 (bottom left)

ISBN
978-1-63517-854-8 (hardcover)
978-1-63517-955-2 (paperback)
978-1-64185-158-9 (ebook pdf)
978-1-64185-057-5 (hosted ebook)

Library of Congress Control Number: 2018931104

Printed in the United States of America
Mankato, MN
May, 2018

About the Author

Nick Rebman enjoys reading, drawing, and traveling to places where he doesn't speak the language. He lives in Minnesota.

Table of Contents

Sharks

Sharks are fish.

Sharks can be many sizes.

Some are small.

Some are big.

A shark has **teeth**.

A shark has **fins**.

A shark has a **tail**.

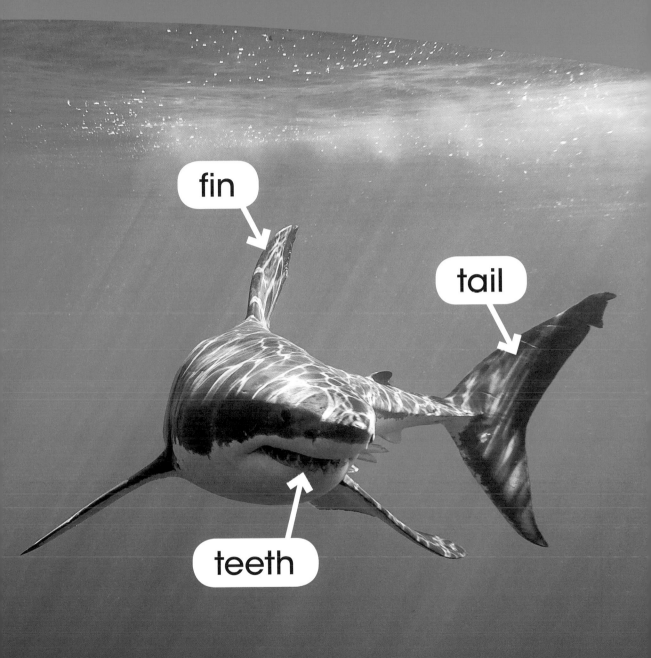

Behavior

Sharks can swim fast.

Sharks can swim far.

Sharks live in the **sea**.

Most sharks live alone.

Food

Sharks hunt for food.

They can smell.

They find fish to eat.

Some sharks live for
20 years.
Some sharks live for
100 years or more.

Glossary

fins

tail

sea

teeth

Index